Jousting with Jesters

This is the story of
Dennis the dragon's quest to find his flame.

Jousting with Jesters

An ABC
for the Younger Dragon

story and illustrations by
Martin Springett

ORCA BOOK PUBLISHERS

A Avoid aunties armed with arrows.

B Beware of barons bringing broadswords to breakfast.

C Careful when passing a capering carnival.

D Dance with dwarves as darkness deepens.

Eagerly eavesdrop on an eagle entertaining elves.

F Faced with a furious fairy, flee, flee, flee!

Gentle giants make generous guides.

H Heavy horses help with homework.

I Ignore irritating imps.

J Joust jauntily with a jolly jester.

K Keep your kit from knaves and knights.

L Leap lightly over lolling leprechauns.

Manage mad magicians with marmalade.

No noise near napping gnomes.

Offer oranges to ogres out of doors.

Please don't pester passing poets.

Queue quietly for queenly quests.

R Run rapidly after the rotten robber.

S Speak special spells speedily.

T Take time to thank a toiling troll.

Unyoke the unruly unicorn!

Verily, vault up the vermillion volcano!

Write the wizard to wake the West Wind.

Xylophones assist exits.

Welcome Dennis
Dragon of Castle Yarrow

Y Yield a yellow flame to youthful yeomen.

As Auntie always says, "Zoom with Zest!"

*This book is for Pauline Baynes,
whom I am proud to call friend and colleague.*

Also for Buddy, our delightfully daft doggy.

*Special thanks to Ken Steacy for his guidance in the digital domain, and to
Terry Findlay & David Shelton for their super support and intriguing insights.*

Thanks to Miriam for her carefully crafted comments on the compositions.

**How many objects can you find on each page of this book that
begin with the page's letter of the alphabet?
Visit www.orcabook.com or www.martinspringett.com
to find out which objects you (or we) have missed.**

Text copyright © 2006 Martin Springett

Illustrations copyright © 2006 Martin Springett

Library and Archives Canada Cataloguing in Publication

Springett, Martin

Jousting with jesters: an ABC for the younger dragon / story and illustrations by Martin Springett.

ISBN 1-55143-327-3

1. English language--Alphabet--Juvenile literature. 2. Alphabet books.

I. Title.

PE1155.S67 2006   j421'.1   C2006-901770-0

First published in the United States 2006

Library of Congress Control Number: 2006924163

Summary: This medieval tale uses the alphabet to guide a young dragon's quest to find his flame.

Orca Book Publishers gratefully acknowledges the support for its publishing programs provided by
the following agencies: the government of Canada through the Book Publishing Industry Development Program,
the Canada Council for the Arts, the government of British Columbia, and the British Columbia Arts Council.

Orca Book Publishers
Box 5626 Stn. B
Victoria, BC Canada
V8R 6S4

Orca Book Publishers
PO Box 468
Custer, WA USA
98240-0468

Printed and bound in Hong Kong
09 08 07 06 • 5 4 3 2 1